s to be returned   for

s to be returned   for

THE OZONE LAYER

© Aladdin Books Ltd 1990

Designed and produced by
Aladdin Books Ltd
70 Old Compton Street
London W1V 5PA

First published in
Great Britain in 1990 by
Franklin Watts Ltd
96 Leonard Street
London EC2A 4RH

ISBN 0 7496 0090 X

A CIP catalogue record for this
book is available from the British
Library.

Printed in Belgium

The publishers would like to
acknowledge that the
photographs reproduced within
this book have been posed by
models or have been obtained
from photographic agencies.

Design	David West Children's Book Design
Editor	Nicholas de Vere
Researcher	Cecilia Weston-Baker
Illustrator	Alex Pang

The author, Dr Tony Hare, is a
writer, ecologist and TV
presenter. He works with several
environmental organisations
including the London Wildlife
Trust, the British Association of
Nature Conservationists and
Plantlife, of which he is Chairman
of the Board.

The consultants: Jacky Karas is a
senior Research Associate at the
Climatic Research Unit at the
University of East Anglia.
Chris Rose is Director of Media
Natura, the organisation that
brings together conservation
groups and the media. He is
environmental consultant to
Greenpeace and Friends of the
Earth.

SAVE OUR EARTH

TONY HARE

GLOUCESTER PRESS

London · New York · Toronto · Sydney

CONTENTS

INTRODUCTION

The Sun, together with the atmosphere – a layer of gases which surrounds the Earth – makes life on our planet possible. Without these the Earth would be a dark frozen planet.

The light from the Sun is used by plants to live and grow. Animals, on the other hand, cannot use the Sun's energy directly, and they depend on plants for food. Without plants there could be no animals, and without the Sun there could be no plants.

But the Sun does not only produce light and heat but also forms of radiation that are harmful to life on Earth. Fortunately, most of this radiation never reaches the ground, because it is intercepted by the atmosphere. The OZONE LAYER – a thin layer of gas miles above our heads – is especially important in filtering out damaging radiation from the Sun.

But now the ozone layer is under threat. Chemicals that can destroy ozone are drifting up into the atmosphere from our homes, factories, towns and cities. And unless we stop this happening, more of the Sun's dangerous radiation could get through – and that could mean ecological disaster.

◄ **The tropical rainforest abounds with lush green plants, ranging from beautiful orchids and ferns to towering trees. The bright light falling on the rainforest, and the warm humid conditions, make the rich and spectacular life of the forest possible. Both the light and warmth are caused by radiation from the Sun which has filtered through the atmosphere.**

THE SUN

The Sun is a star and is at the centre of the Solar System. It is a ball of burning gases spinning through space. More than a million times larger than the Earth, the Sun is extremely hot. Its surface temperature is about 6,000°C, and deep in its heart, the temperature is an amazing 15 million °C. Nuclear reactions within the Sun's hot core create the energy that makes the Sun shine. Changing dark spots on the face of the Sun and violent flares, millions of kilometres high, show that the Sun is always active.

The Sun is our nearest star and produces light and heat for us on Earth. Both light and heat are forms of radiation from the Sun. Radiation is a way of transferring energy from one place to another, usually travelling in straight lines called rays.

▼ The Solar System is made up of the Sun, nine known planets (several of which have moons), and a band of rocks called the asteroid belt. The planets and the asteroid belt orbit the Sun. The planets vary greatly in size and distance from the Sun, but all are small in relation to the Sun.

Key
1 Inner planets (Mercury, Venus, Earth, Mars)
2 Asteroid belt
3 Jupiter
4 Saturn
5 Uranus
6 Neptune
7 Pluto

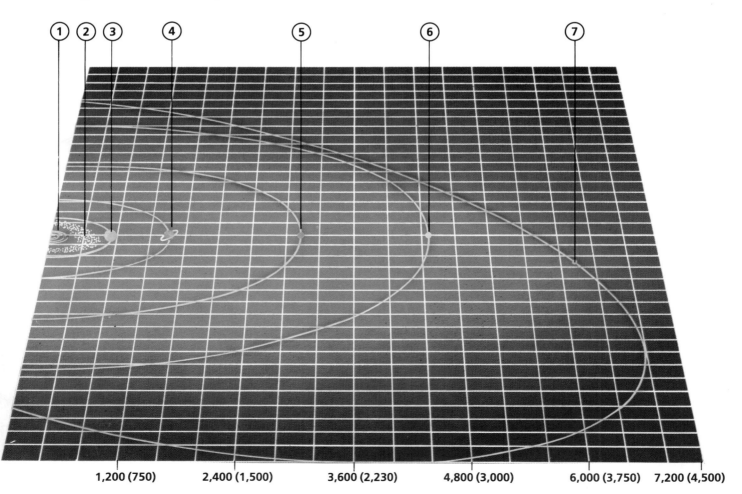

| 1,200 (750) | 2,400 (1,500) | 3,600 (2,230) | 4,800 (3,000) | 6,000 (3,750) | 7,200 (4,500) |

SCALE: Km (Mi) in millions

Light is the only type of radiation that humans can see, and the light we can see coming from the Sun is called "white light". This visible light is, however, a small part of a much larger family of radiation, called the "electromagnetic spectrum". All types of electromagnetic radiation travel from the Sun through space at the same speed, 300,000km per second – the "speed of light". At one end of the spectrum are gamma rays, X-rays and ultra-violet light; at the other, infra-red rays, microwaves and radio waves.

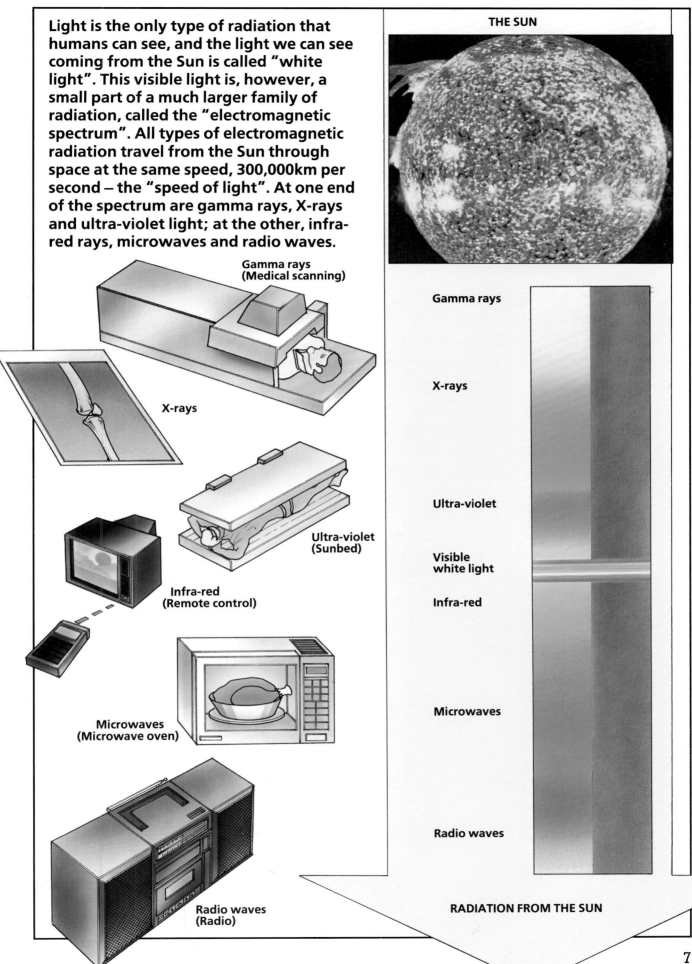

THE SUN

Gamma rays
(Medical scanning)

X-rays

Ultra-violet
(Sunbed)

Infra-red
(Remote control)

Microwaves
(Microwave oven)

Radio waves
(Radio)

Gamma rays

X-rays

Ultra-violet

Visible
white light

Infra-red

Microwaves

Radio waves

RADIATION FROM THE SUN

THE EARTH

The Earth is the third nearest planet to the Sun, and is the only planet that has the right conditions for life. Other planets would be too hot or too cold, or have air that would be poisonous.

On the Earth we are about 150 million kilometres away from the Sun. Only a tiny fraction of the Sun's energy actually gets through our atmosphere and reaches the surface. A lot of the rays are either absorbed by the atmosphere or reflected back into space.

All living things rely on the energy from the Sun. The rays that get through provide a temperature on Earth in which life can exist. Plants use sunlight in a process called photosynthesis, which allows them to absorb and convert the Sun's energy for growth. Plants are the basis of food webs. Grazing animals, from caterpillars to cows, eat the plants, and then other animals eat the grazing animals – and all of them breathe oxygen which the plants produce.

▼ Photosynthesis
The olive trees (left) and wildflowers are examples of plants that use the Sun's energy to grow. Their leaves take in carbon dioxide from the air and their roots absorb water from the soil. In photosynthesis, plants use the energy of sunlight to convert these simple substances into sugars and starches and to produce oxygen.

SOLAR RADIATION

Both visible and invisible radiation have travelled vast distances before they reach us, thus losing energy on their journey. When radiation does reach the Earth's atmosphere, some is reflected and some is absorbed by the atmosphere. Then the clouds themselves reflect and absorb some more of the radiation. On a clear day without clouds we are able to feel the strength of the Sun's rays. Finally the ground reflects or absorbs the radiation that has travelled through space, and through the atmosphere.

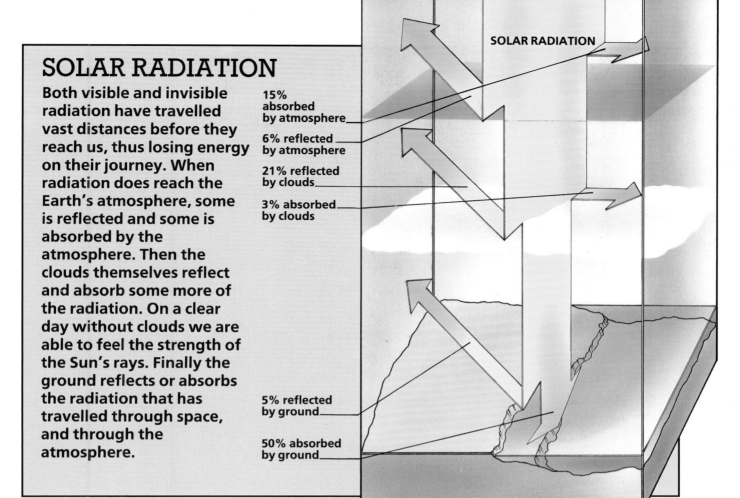

SOLAR RADIATION

15% absorbed by atmosphere

6% reflected by atmosphere

21% reflected by clouds

3% absorbed by clouds

5% reflected by ground

50% absorbed by ground

► The food web

A food web is made up of several food chains that interlink. All living things depend on other living things for survival. Animals that eat plants are called herbivores. Animals that eat herbivores are called carnivores, who may in turn be eaten by other carnivores. Through photosynthesis, the Sun feeds the plants. These may then be eaten by cows, caterpillars, rabbits or man. At the ends of the food chains are the predators – the bird, the fox and man himself.

SUNLIGHT

KEY

1 Plants	5 Predatory bird
2 Rabbit	6 Fox
3 Caterpillar	7 Man
4 Blackbird	8 Cow

THE ATMOSPHERE

Our planet Earth is surrounded by layers of gas. These make up what we call the atmosphere. The Earth's atmosphere is invisible, but it is vital to our existence. It is mainly composed of a gas called nitrogen. The oxygen we need to breathe makes up just 23% of the atmosphere. Between them nitrogen and oxygen make up about 99% of the Earth's atmosphere.

The atmosphere is about 700km deep. The air gradually gets thinner at higher altitudes until eventually there is no atmosphere at all – beyond the atmosphere is outer space.

There are other gases in the atmosphere which play a vital role, even though they are there only in tiny amounts. Called "greenhouse gases", they allow the Sun's energy to reach the Earth, but stop heat from the Earth being released into space. They trap the heat near the Earth's surface.

▼ **This satellite picture of a section of the Earth (north-east Africa and the Middle East are clearly visible) shows the clouds in the atmosphere that surround the Earth.**

ATMOSPHERE

The atmosphere is a thin layer of gases around the Earth. "Atmosphere" is Greek for circle of vapour. Within the atmosphere itself there are different layers – the higher you go the less the air.

Aurora [6]
This is a layer where glowing coloured lights – auroras – are sometimes seen in the skies of the North and South poles. Particles from the Sun run into the gases in the Earth's atmosphere, causing a glow.

Thermosphere [5]
In this layer meteors arriving from space break up upon their contact with the atmosphere.

Dust belt [4]
A layer of dust particles formed from the descending meteors that have broken up.

Stratosphere [3]
This extends up to about 50km above Earth. The temperature, though below freezing, rises the further up you travel.

Ozone layer [2]
This contains the ozone that absorbs most of the ultra-violet radiation before it reaches the Earth.

Troposphere [1]
This contains the air we breathe; clouds, rain and snow all form in this layer.

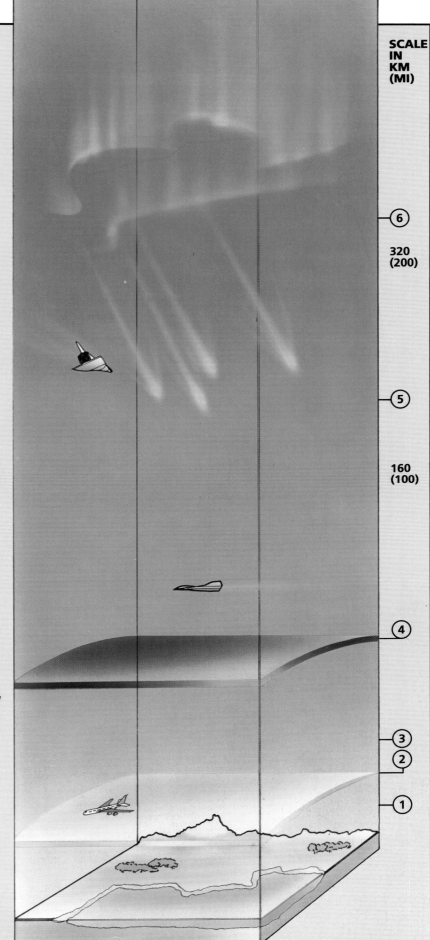

SCALE IN KM (MI)

6

320 (200)

5

160 (100)

4

3

2

1

11

THE OZONE LAYER

Ozone is a form of oxygen. It is created when ultra-violet radiation from the Sun meets oxygen in the atmosphere. The ozone layer occurs throughout the stratosphere but is most dense between about 20 and 30 km above the ground. It absorbs most of the dangerous ultra-violet radiation reaching the Earth from the Sun. The ultra-violet that does get through to the surface of the Earth has important effects. It is the radiation which gives people their natural skin colouring. But too much ultra-violet radiation can have harmful effects on plants and animals including humans.

▼ **Many people take their holidays in hot and sunny climates. They spend long periods lying in the Sun, absorbing the Sun's radiation and often getting burnt. They receive some ultra-violet radiation, but most has been absorbed by the ozone layer.**

The ozone layer in balance

The way ultra-violet radiation, ozone, oxygen and other chemicals act together in the atmosphere is extremely complicated, but under normal circumstances everything is in balance. Ozone is being made and broken down all the time in the atmosphere. The amount of ozone in the atmosphere stays more or less the same.

The threat to the ozone layer comes from pollutants which can destroy the ozone, and this upsets the balance in the atmosphere. The amount of dangerous ultra-violet radiation reaching the Earth may increase should the balance be disturbed in the ozone layer.

Ultra-violet radiation is one of the "rays" that we receive from the Sun. It travels through space into the atmosphere, until it reaches the ozone layer.

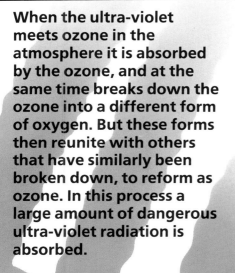

When the ultra-violet meets ozone in the atmosphere it is absorbed by the ozone, and at the same time breaks down the ozone into a different form of oxygen. But these forms then reunite with others that have similarly been broken down, to reform as ozone. In this process a large amount of dangerous ultra-violet radiation is absorbed.

Ozone layer

⬡ Ozone
▷ Oxygen

Ultra-violet radiation

Once the ultra-violet radiation has been filtered by the ozone, a reduced amount penetrates the remaining atmosphere to reach the surface of the Earth.

13

THE OZONE-EATERS

Scientists expect the Sun to keep shining for at least another 200 million years. The Earth has its parasol of gas – the atmosphere – to protect it from the dangerous radiation that the Sun produces. But, unfortunately, the composition of the atmsophere is changing as a result of human activity.

Part of the atmosphere – the ozone layer – is under threat from chemicals that we use on Earth. The guilty chemicals are chlorofluorocarbons (often called CFCs for short). They can last for more than 100 years in the atmosphere, slowly moving up through the atmosphere before breaking down to produce the chemicals that destroy the ozone layer. Although the best-known culprits are CFCs, which are the most important of the ozone-destroying chemicals, other chemicals can also help to break ozone down. On Earth these chemicals are inert – they never change, and nothing happens when they meet other chemicals. But very slowly they drift up into the atmosphere. When they get high enough into the atmosphere something does happen to them – ultra-violet light from the Sun breaks them down and changes them.

What are CFCs
CFCs are chemicals called chlorofluorocarbons. They have a number of applications. They are used in a variety of aerosols, refrigerators, some air-conditioning systems and some packaging materials.

The way CFCs react with ultra-violet and ozone in the ozone layer is complicated. When the CFCs reach the ozone layer, the ultra-violet strikes the CFC and releases chlorine from it. This reacts with the ozone, breaking up ozone into different forms of oxygen. The chlorine itself remains unchanged, so it continues to destroy ozone, turning it into different forms of oxygen, over and over again.

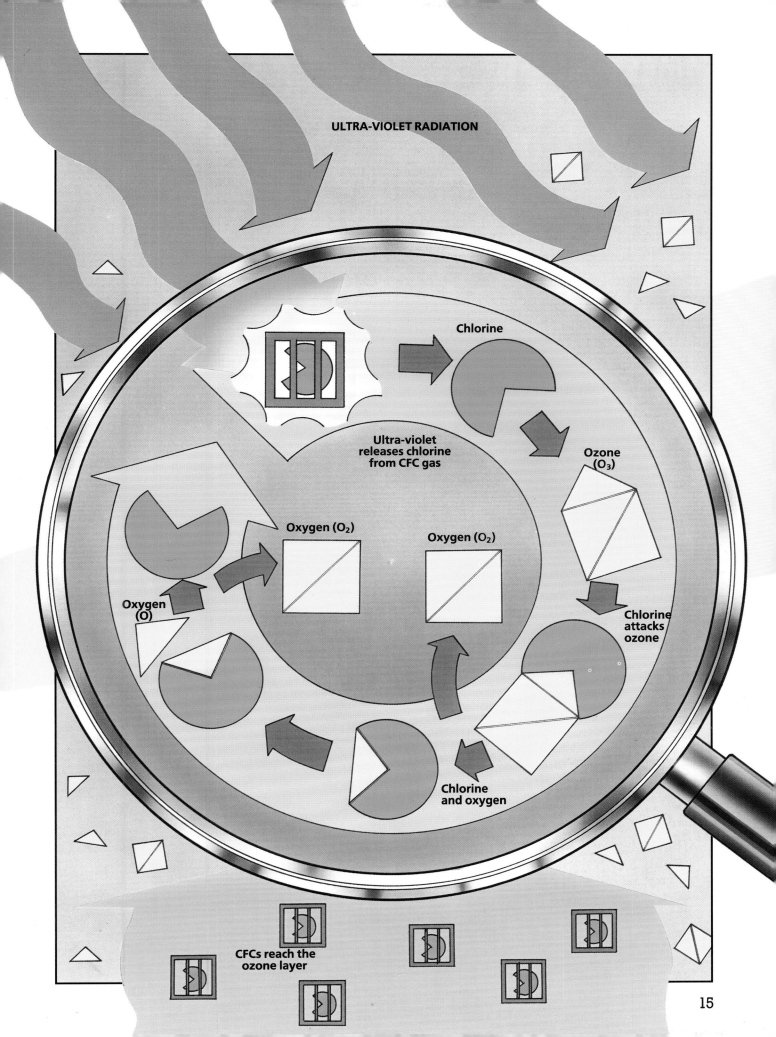

ULTRA-VIOLET RADIATION

Chlorine

Ultra-violet releases chlorine from CFC gas

Ozone (O₃)

Oxygen (O₂)

Oxygen (O₂)

Oxygen (O)

Chlorine attacks ozone

Chlorine and oxygen

CFCs reach the ozone layer

15

WHERE THEY COME FROM

Ozone-eaters come from a variety of sources. Aerosols are made for all sorts of personal and household uses. Hairsprays, anti-perspirants, fly spray and paint-spray are all aerosols and all use CFCs. In the UK alone, 800 million aersols were used last year. CFCs are used in the manufacture of some types of foam packaging where they are used to expand it. Sometimes CFCs remain trapped in the bubbles of foam packaging and escape when it is crushed and burned.

In fridges and some air-conditioning units, especially those used in cars in hot climates, CFCs are used as the cooling fluid that circulates to keep the temperature down.

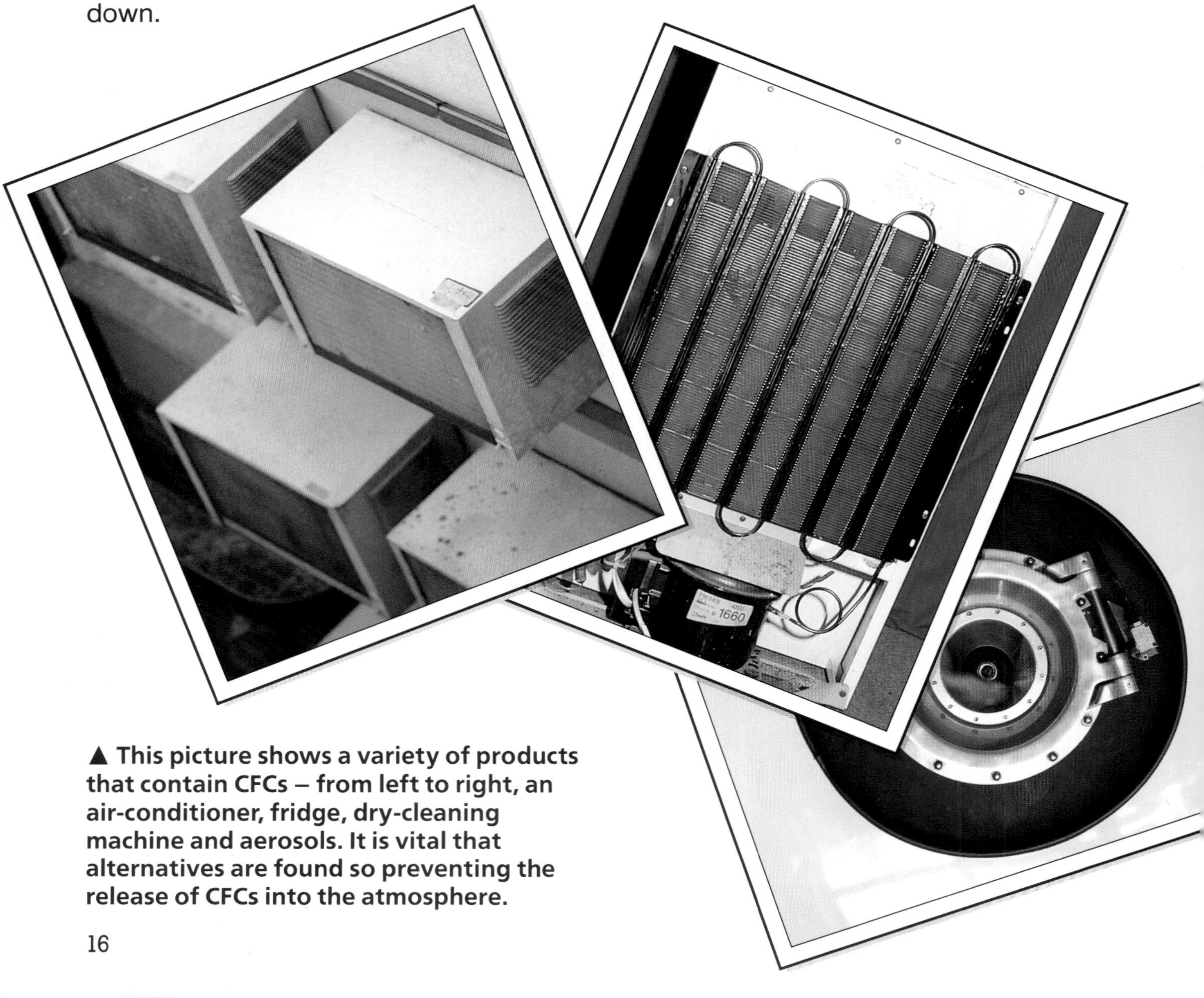

▲ **This picture shows a variety of products that contain CFCs – from left to right, an air-conditioner, fridge, dry-cleaning machine and aerosols. It is vital that alternatives are found so preventing the release of CFCs into the atmosphere.**

All the other ozone-eaters

Ozone-threatening gases do not only come from these sources. The factories that make aerosols also release CFCs into the atmosphere. And other chemicals threaten the ozone layer too, such as carbon tetrachloride – a chemical used in the manufacture of CFCs, and sold in some countries as a solvent – even though it has been banned in many places because it has been connected with liver cancer. Halons, which are used in fire extinguishers, are ozone-eaters, and another is methylchloroform, which is used as a solvent. Solvents are used in many products which we use every day, such as glues and spirit-based pens, and in paints. And trichloroethane is used in typist's correction fluid.

▲ **This industrial complex produces chemicals.**

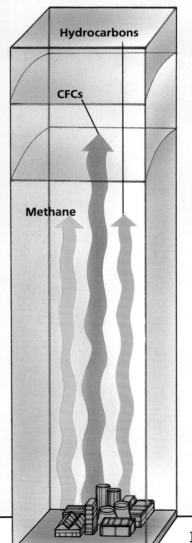

CFCs

CFCs, and the other chemicals that are endangering the ozone layer, take time to drift up into the ozone layer. They may also last a very long time – most, for 70-110 years and in some cases up to 23,000 years. They also drift higher than other substances like methane and hydro-carbons. Because of this scientists find it difficult to predict what damage is likely to result ultimately.

Hydrocarbons

CFCs

Methane

17

THE HOLE

At certain times every year, over Antarctica, the levels of ozone in the ozone layer fall drastically. There is an area where the layer is so sparse that there is virtually a hole.

During the Antarctic spring, which is at the same time as our autumn, there are some areas over Antarctica where as much as 40% of the ozone has disappeared in some years. The hole is as big as North America and as deep as Mount Everest.

Records show that the levels of ozone in the Antarctic atmosphere do vary naturally from year to year. But the hole has been observed in recent years to be greater than that which occurs naturally. Scientists have collected samples from the atmosphere where the hole occurs, and have found high levels of ozone-eating chemicals. These are almost certainly responsible for the hole.

The hole in the Antarctic
Scientists use high-level reconnaissance aircraft, balloons and satellites to gather their information. This satellite picture (right) shows quite clearly the hole that is appearing in the ozone over the Antarctic pole. The blackish area in the middle confirms the existence of a hole. No hole has yet been found over the Arctic, although the chemicals that could cause it are present. But the ozone layer has certainly been found to thin out over the northern hemisphere in general. In a band that stretches around the globe in the latitudes between Nottingham and the Orkneys, up to 7% ozone depletion has been found in winter.

▲ This NASA ER-2 high-altitude aircraft is being prepared for flight.

▶ Satellites orbit regularly over the Arctic and Antarctic, taking pictures of the Earth with sophisticated cameras.

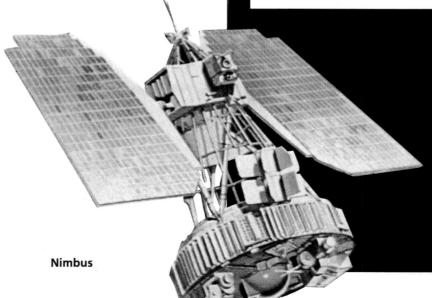

Nimbus

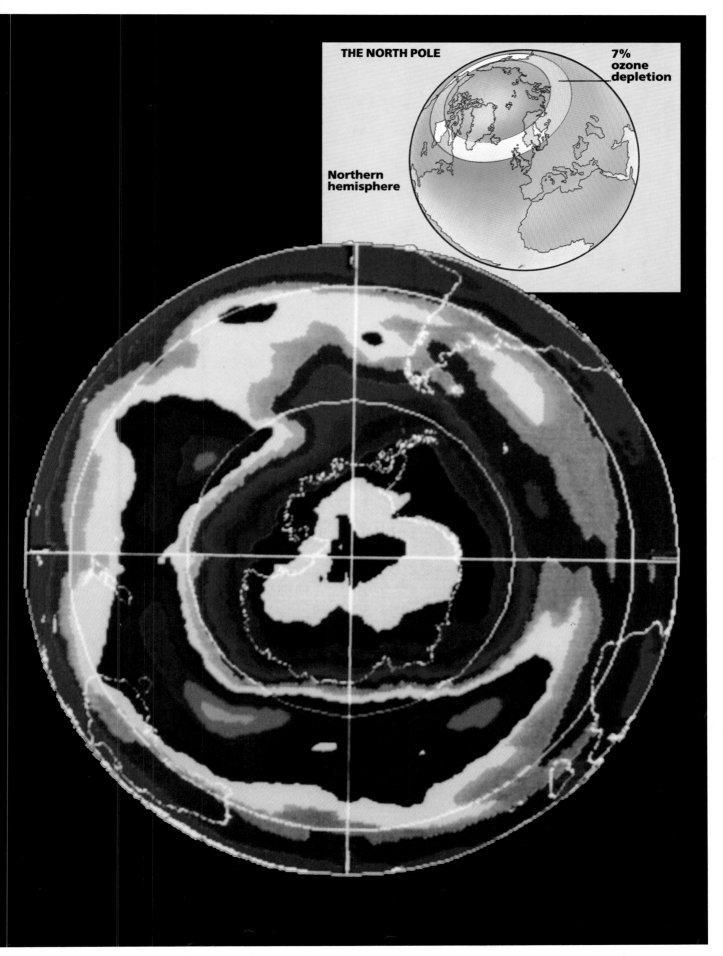

THE NORTH POLE

7% ozone depletion

Northern hemisphere

WHAT COULD HAPPEN

The ozone layer absorbs most of the dangerous ultra-violet radiation. If more of this radiation got through it would cause an increase in skin cancer and cataracts – a major cause of blindness in the countries where modern medical treatment is unavailable. It has been estimated that a 1% depletion of the ozone layer would result in an extra 70,000 cases of skin cancer every year worldwide. But the increased ultra-violet radiation would not just affect us – it would affect all life on Earth. There would be damage to crops, and damage to the plants and trees that form the basis of the food chains that support life on Earth. So there would be a threat to the world's food supply. In the sea, if the plankton – tiny plants and animals in the surface waters, were killed, the fish would starve, the seas would die, and a major source of human food resources would be lost.

▼ Plankton (see photo inset) is the basis of the food chain in the sea. Plankton consists of tiny plants and animals, and is eaten by marine creatures such as fish and squid. The bigger fish and sea mammals eat other fish. The Baleen whales such as the Blue whale, the Humpback whale, and Gray whale (below), bypass the chain and feed directly on large amounts of plankton.

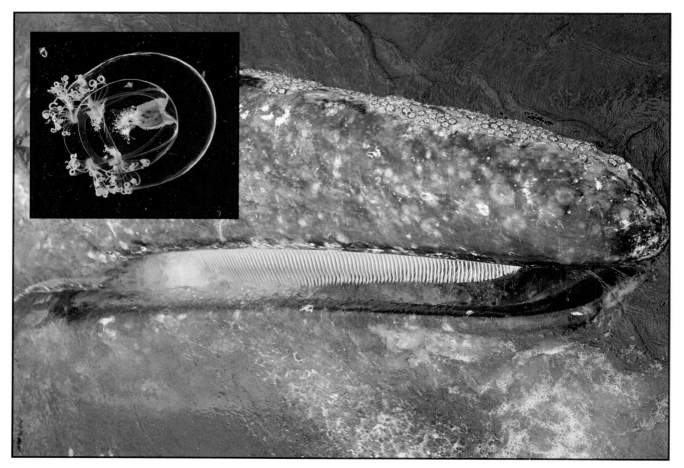

PHOTOCHEMICAL SMOG

Increased ultra-violet radiation reaching the Earth could raise the likelihood of photochemical smog over heavily built-up areas. Smog is formed when ultra-violet radiation strikes air pollution produced by cars.

_____ Ultra-violet radiation

Smog

ALTERNATIVES

Risking the destruction of the ozone layer is unnecessary. There are alternatives for virtually all the uses of CFCs. For example, aerosol sprays which use CFCs can be replaced by harmless pump-action sprays which do no damage to the environment. Moreover, foam-packaging insulation material can be made without the use of CFCs. People are beginning to wonder whether we really need all the packaging that goods come in – a lot of it is only decoration and serves no useful purpose anyway. The CFCs in fridges can be recycled – they can be sucked out of an old fridge and put into a new one.

"Release of CFCs could be prevented if consumers and businesses were offered cash incentives to return broken-down air conditioners and refrigerators to auto and appliance dealers. Then the units could be sent back to the manufacturers so that the CFCs could be reused."

Time January 1989

"Much of what reaches the atmosphere is not coming from industrial sources. It's things like sloppy handling of hamburger containers."

Senator Albert Gore of Tennessee, USA

"It has also been suggested that environmentally-damaging substances like CFCs should be made more expensive to encourage recycling and a switch to less harmful alternatives."

Which? October 1989

► While the developed and heavily industrialised countries of the world can afford to look at the long-term dangers of a thinning of the ozone layer, the problems of developing countries are very different. Their priorities lean towards the provision of basic food supplies, and a general increase in their standard of living. Whereas refrigerators and aerosol sprays are common-place items in a developed country, they are often luxury items in developing ones. It is therefore difficult for developing countries to accept that they are not entitled to such luxury items, and it is harder for them to agree to ban CFCs.

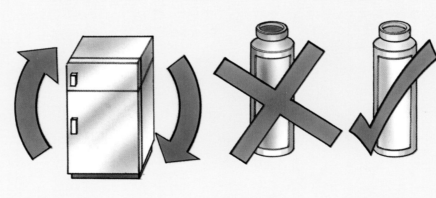

Banning CFCs
To protect the ozone layer it will ultimately be vital to ban harmful CFCs on a worldwide basis. Even now manufacturers are beginning to look for alternatives. There is growing opposition to the general use of CFCs worldwide.

Recycling fridges
The disposal of fridges is a major problem. By leaving them on a tip or by crushing them, the CFCs are released into the atmosphere. It is now possible to extract the CFCs from fridge containers and to recycle or store them.

Alternative gases
Not only can the CFCs in some cases be recycled, but they can also be replaced by other chemicals and gases. CO_2 is now widely used for foam fire-extinguishers. Others can be replaced by harmless pump-action sprays.

WHAT'S BEING DONE

In September 1987 many countries signed an agreement called the Montreal Protocol. They promised to cut back the production of CFCs by half, by the end of the century.

It is now realised that the situation was worse than people imagined and that the Protocol did not go far enough. It is now under review. If the ozone layer is to survive, then many scientists believe that the countries must agree to reduce their CFC production to zero by the end of the century. Scientists are discovering more and more ozone-destroyers all the time. If the ozone layer is to be maintained we must plan for the future and completely stop using all the ozone-destroyers. It is vital that all countries work together to provide the goods people want, without destroying our environment.

▶ **Some products such as aerosols have symbols printed on the can to inform you the propellant is not harmful to the ozone layer. However alternative propellants are often greenhouse gases, and add to the greenhouse effect. The safest are pump-action sprays.**

▼ **Margaret Thatcher, the Prime Minister of Great Britain, speaks out at a conference on the ozone layer, organised to protect the environment.**

▶ **In this Greenpeace demonstration outside a well-known West German chemical factory, protesters are demanding an end to the production of CFCs.**

Hoechs
zerstört die Ozo

WIR BRINGEN DIE
POLE ZUM SCHMELZEN

WIR B
POLE ZU

OZONE FRIENDLY

300 ml ℮

CONTAINS NO CHLORO-FLUOROCARBON PROPELLANT ALLEGED TO DAMAGE THE OZONE LAYER

Sofortiger Stopp der FCKW-Produktion!
Minister Töpfer, handeln oder gehen Sie!

GREENPEACE

TAKING ACTION

Organisations like Greenpeace and Friends of the Earth (FOE) are aiming campaigns at consumers, industry and governments, to try to alert them to the great dangers of pollution and to encourage them to help protect the ozone layer. These organisations demonstrate outside government buildings and factories to voice their concern. This is already having considerable effect. Manufacturers are influenced by public opinion, and are beginning to cut down the use of CFCs in their products.

It also helps when prominent people like Prince Charles refuse to use CFC aerosols because of the damage they cause.

WHAT YOU CAN DO

The ozone layer may be miles above our heads, but there are things that we can all do to help save it.

● – Buy only "ozone-friendly" aerosols, or pump-action sprays.

● – Try not to buy packaging that uses CFCs. Not all foam packaging does contain CFCs, but try asking the person selling it to you before you buy it.

● – A dumped fridge leaks its CFCs into the air. Take it to one of the shops that recycles fridge CFCs, or to the local recycling depot.

Useful addresses:

Greenpeace UK
30-31 Islington Green
London
N1 8XE
Tel: 01-359 7396

Friends of the Earth
26-28 Underwood St
London
N1 7JQ
Tel: 01-490 4547

Campaign for Lead Free Air
3 Endsleigh St
London
WC1H 0DD
Tel: 0273 601312

The Environment Council
80 York Way
London
N1 9AG
Tel: 01 278 4736

Make a poster
One of the most important things that can be done is to make more people aware of the ozone crisis. One way you can do this is to make a poster to hang up on a school notice board or in your bedroom.

1) Think up a striking or clever heading for the poster which will catch the attention of the viewers.

2) Design an illustration or symbol like the one shown here or cut pictures out of magazines and make a montage that conveys the main message.

3) Read through this book and try to summarise in about 30-40 words what is happening to the ozone layer and why it is important.

4) Again by reading through the book, make some suggestions as to what can be done to help save the ozone layer.

5) Include some other information if there is room – such as useful addresses to contact for more information, and symbols that are printed on ozone-friendly items.

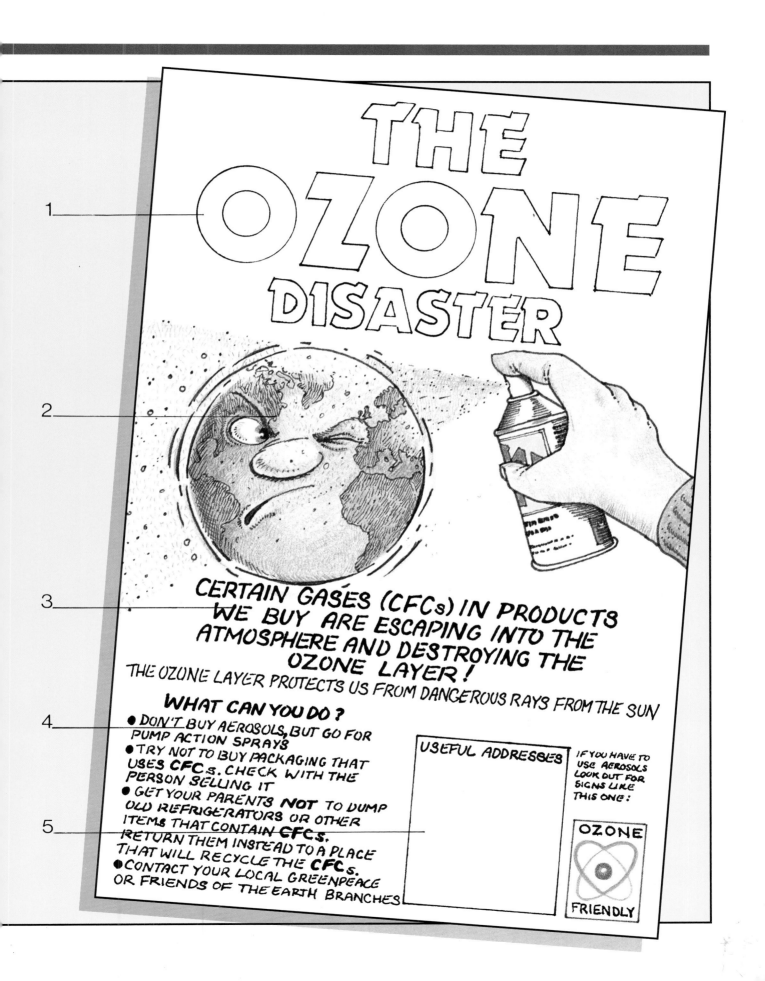

FACT FILE 1

How big is the ozone layer

The ozone layer spreads right out over a thick layer of atmosphere. But if you brought it down to Earth, to ground level, where there is a lot more air above it to press it down, it would only be about 3mm thick.

CFCs and the greenhouse effect

CFCs do not just threaten the ozone layer. They are also greenhouse gases. This means that they help trap heat close to the Earth's surface. Greenhouse gases cause the greenhouse effect, which is responsible for keeping the earth warm. It is also responsible for a gradual increase in temperatures throughout the world. Global warming could have devastating effects on climate, sea level, crop production and wildlife. Although they are present in smaller quantities than the best known greenhouse gas – carbon dioxide – some CFCs are more than 10,000 times as powerful. All the more reason to stop using them as soon as possible.

The origin of the ozone layer

The Sun's ultra-violet radiation plays a vital role in maintaining the ozone layer. When the Sun's ultra-violet hits the atmosphere it meets oxygen and causes a chemical reaction to take place which forms ozone. Oxygen exists as molecules which are made up of atoms – an oxygen molecule is made up of two oxygen atoms. When the ultra-violet strikes an oxygen molecule it splits it in two. The end result is that some ultra-violet radiation has been stopped from getting any further, and two oxygen atoms are free in the atmosphere. A single oxygen atom may meet another oxygen atom, and the two may join to form an oxygen molecule; or it may bump into an oxygen molecule, and join up with it to make a molecule with three atoms – ozone. Then, when ultra-violet strikes the ozone molecule, it breaks it up again, setting the oxygen atom free in the atmosphere. In this way, some of the ultra-violet has been prevented from reaching the Earth.

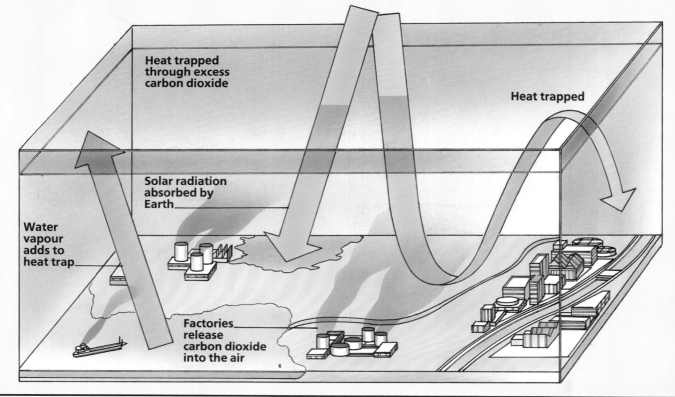

Heat trapped through excess carbon dioxide

Heat trapped

Solar radiation absorbed by Earth

Water vapour adds to heat trap

Factories release carbon dioxide into the air

For an oxygen molecule and an oxygen atom to combine to make ozone, a catalyst (normally nitrogen) needs to be present. Ozone is being made and destroyed all the time, and most of the ultra-violet radiation is being stopped from reaching the surface of the Earth. But when the ozone-destroyers are involved, there is more ozone being broken down than made.

HOW OZONE IS MADE

Oxygen (O_2) molecule

Catalyst

oxygen (O) atom

Ozone (O_3)

How can scientists tell that the ozone layer is under attack?

An instrument called a spectrophotometer, shows them how much radiation is getting through. When they see that there is more ultra-violet getting through than there should be, they know that there has been a reduction in the amount of ozone in the ozone layer.

What do CFCs do?

When CFCs are used in aerosols, they act as the propellant mixed with the product – they are put in the tin under pressure, and when you press the button they force the product out.

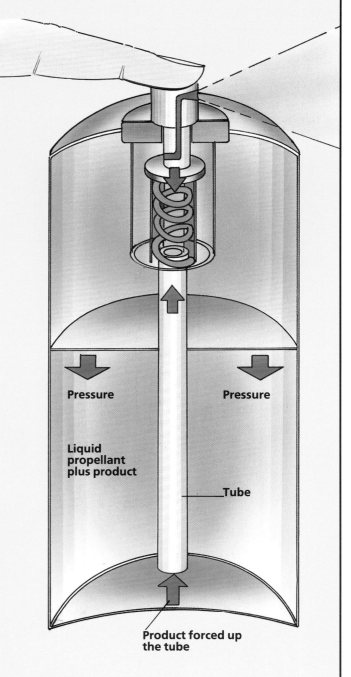

Pressure

Pressure

Liquid propellant plus product

Tube

Product forced up the tube

Unfriendly replacements

Some manufacturers are replacing the CFCs in aerosols with other gases. The cans are often labelled "ozone friendly". The gases used – hydrocarbons – may be safe for the ozone layer, but they are greenhouse gases. So they – like the CFCs – are bad for the environment. The only really environment-friendly spray is a pump-action one.

Useful radiation

The Sun's radiation has many uses apart from photosynthesis. Along with the little infra-red radiation that gets through, it helps to keep the planet warm. Light in the visible spectrum allows us to see. Radio waves that come through from the Sun and other more distant stars are used in the science of radio astronomy. This helps scientists find out about distant galaxies. We can put radiation similar to that produced by the Sun to many different uses. Infra-red radiation can be used in burglar alarms. Even radiation that is dangerous to life on Earth can be put to valuable use. Ultra-violet is used in health lamps, and X-rays in hospitals.

Marine food chains

About 70% of our Earth is covered by the seas, and there are food chains in the seas as well as on land. In the upper parts, the Sun's light penetrates far enough for tiny plants and animals to live in the surface waters. They are called plankton. Some of the seas' great giants, such as manta rays and many whales, eat plankton. The fish that we eat also depend on the plankton, either directly or indirectly.

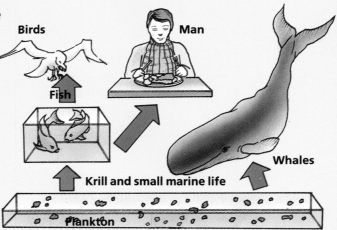

Birds

Man

Fish

Whales

Krill and small marine life

Plankton

GLOSSARY

CFCs/chlorofluorocarbons – Chemicals which are used for a variety of applications, for instance, in aerosols, in fridges and in the manufacture of foam packaging.

Electromagnetic spectrum – The whole range of known types of radiation. All of them travel at the speed of light – 300,000 km per second – and usually travel in straight lines.

Food chains – A chain of plants and animals which act as food for each other. For example, caterpillars eat leaves, small birds eat caterpillars and birds of prey eat small birds.

Food web – All living things depend on each other, either directly or indirectly. Most animals and plants take part in more than one food chain. Caterpillars, for example, are eaten by many different types of birds and also by some small mammals. So the way all food chains mesh together is called a food web.

Greenhouse warming – Atmospheric pollution has increased the greenhouse effect by putting more gases that trap heat into the atmosphere. This could cause the Earth's temperature to rise.

Greenhouse effect – Some gases in the atmosphere let the Sun's rays through to warm the Earth, but do not allow the radiation coming back to pass through. This keeps the atmosphere – and the planet – warm. It is known as the greenhouse effect and helps make life on Earth possible.

Montreal Protocol – An international agreement, signed by many countries, which is designed to help save the ozone layer. The countries that signed are taking the necessary actions to cut and prevent pollution.

Ozone – A colourless gas (with a pungent smell) which is a form of oxygen.

Ozone layer – A band of ozone in the atmosphere which stops dangerous ultra-violet light from reaching the Earth's surface.

Radiation – A way of transferring energy from one place to another, for example, from the Sun to the Earth. Most radiation is invisible, but light is an exception and it enables us to see. Other types of radiation include infra-red radiation, X-rays and radio waves.

Ultra-violet radiation – Invisible radiation which causes suntans. It is produced by the Sun. It can also cause skin cancer, however.

INDEX

Photographic Credits:
Cover and page 21: Robert Harding Library; intro page and pages 8 left and right, 17 top and 23: Hutchison Library; pages 7, 18 left, 26 and 29: Science Photo Library; page 10: NASA; pages 14, 16 all, 17 bottom and 25 top: Roger Vlitos; pages 19, 24 and 25 right: Frank Spooner Agency; page 20 left and right: Planet Earth; page 25 top: Greenpeace Communications.